The heavens declare the Glory of God; and the firmament sheweth his handiwork. Ps 91:1

...ng, we ...or is as good as ours. — confident that He's (God is) know that what we've asked 1 John 5:15

This Prayer Journal Belongs to:

The prayer of a person living right with God is ... powerful...
James 5:16b

I Have A Star, Guided Prayer Journal, Freshwater Press ISBN# 978-1-893555-70-9

Once upon a time a beautiful baby was born. That baby was you.

You were born with a Destiny and a promising future. You were born with a star over you that lets the world know that you are here.

Your star also leads your destiny helpers, and destiny friends to you.

Congratulations! It's a bright and shining star. You have a promising future.

But your star is of interest to haters. So, do not let anyone mess with or take your star.

cripture

For I know the thoughts that I think toward you, saith the LORD, thoughts of peace, and not of evil, to give you an expected end. Jeremiah 29:11

What's in your Star?

You purpose is in your star.

Your future is in your star.

Your education is in your star.

Your career is in your star.

Your success is in your star.

Divine favor is in your star.

Your health is in your star.

Your marriage is in your star.

Your wealth is in your star.

Your children are in your star.

The glorious blueprint of your life is in your star.

cripture

Sometimes people you don't even know or people you would never suspect could be jealous of your star.

Do not brag.
Do not tell all your business to everyone.
Be wise.

You got a full scholarship to university. Good. Keep it to yourself. Others may mention it, but don't seek glory for yourself, it can draw evil and jealous people to you.

cripture

Jesus replied, "If I glorify myself, my glory means nothing. My Father, whom you claim as your God, is the one who glorifies me. John 8:54 NIV

_____/_____/_____

I have a Star & I have discovered that I am very good at…
and it might just be my life's work…

Scripture

___/___/___

PURPOSE
What is the reason I am on Earth?

Scripture

To every *thing there is* a season, and a time to every purpose under the heaven: Ecclesiastes 3:1

_____/_____/_____

Will I reach my Destiny?
I would like to be…

Scripture

Prayer

___/___/___

Scripture

___/___/___

Are my friends and family trustworthy?

cripture

A man who has friends must himself be friendly, But there is a friend who sticks closer than a brother. Proverbs 18:24

___/___/___

Prayer & Praise Report

____/____/____

Is My Star At Risk?

Risks include, evil foundation, ancestral covenants, star hunters, star exchangers, jealous household witchcraft, unfriendly friends, occultic people that you may visit for "entertainment", dream defilement, sex in the dream, and sex with anyone who is not your God-ordained spouse.

When your star is especially bright, and your destiny is especially awesome, do not take it lightly.

cripture

Joseph's brothers were jealous of him because of his awesome dream. Genesis 37:11...

Prayer

___/___/___

Scripture

_____/_____/_____

Whoever Takes Your Virginity Could also Take Your Star

Anyone you have sex with who you are not legally married to can steal, dim, or fragment your star.
Ask the young man with a very bright future who had sex with a strange woman and his favor turned sour immediately for a decade! Until he realized it and prayed!!!

cripture

___/___/___

Prayer & Praise Report

____/____/____

Prayer of Salvation

Lord Jesus, I believe You are the Son of God and that you came to Earth and died on the Cross. On the third day, God raised You from the dead.

I confess my sins to You and ask for Your forgiveness.

Please come into my heart as my Lord and Savior. Take complete control of my life and help me to walk in Your footsteps daily.

Thank You Lord for saving me and for answering my prayer

cripture

If you declare with your mouth, "Jesus is Lord," and believe in your heart that God raised him from the dead, you will be saved. Romans 10:9 NIV

____/____/____

Do you have Spiritual Gifts?

You may want to take a Spiritual Gifts Assessment to discover your Spiritual Gifts.

Scripture

For to one is given by the Spirit the word of wisdom; to another the word of knowledge by the same Spirit; To another faith by the same Spirit; to another the gifts of healing by the same Spirit; To another the working of miracles; to another prophecy; to another discerning of spirits; to another *divers* kinds of tongues; to another the interpretation of tongues:
1 Cor 12:8-10

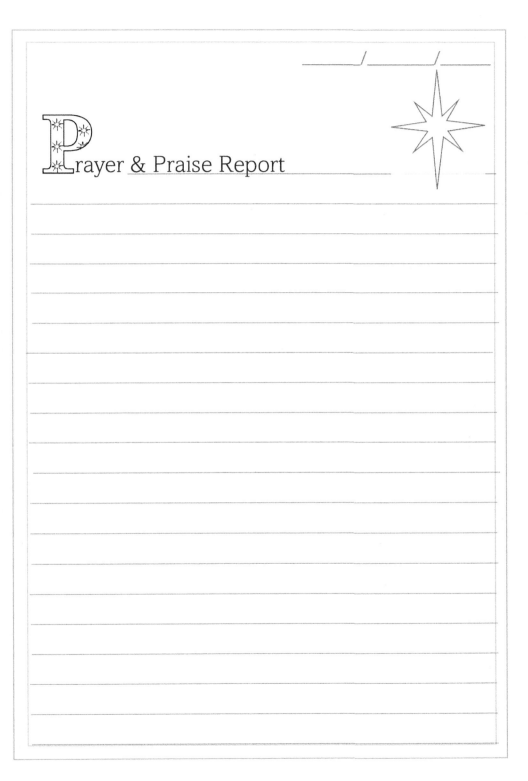

_____/_____/_____

How do your Spiritual Gifts line up with your life's goals?

You may want to take a Spiritual Gifts Assessment to discover your Spiritual Gifts.

cripture

Prayer

_____/_____/_____

Scripture

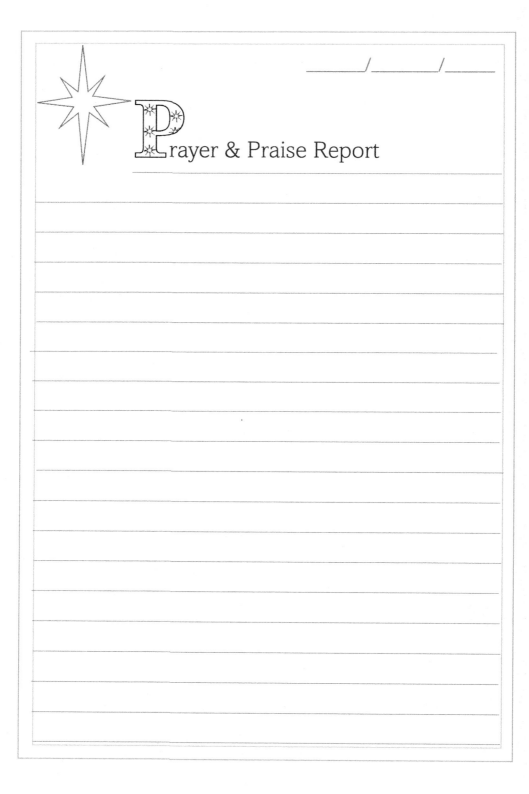

___/___/___

Prayer & Praise Report

What Did God Say?
Did You Hear From God?

_____/_____/_____

Scripture

And a stranger will they not follow, but will flee from him: for they know not the voice of strangers. John 10:5

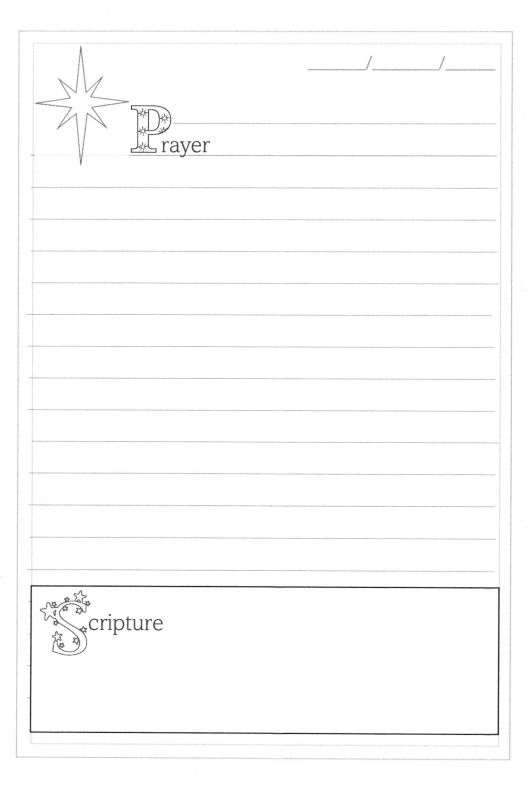

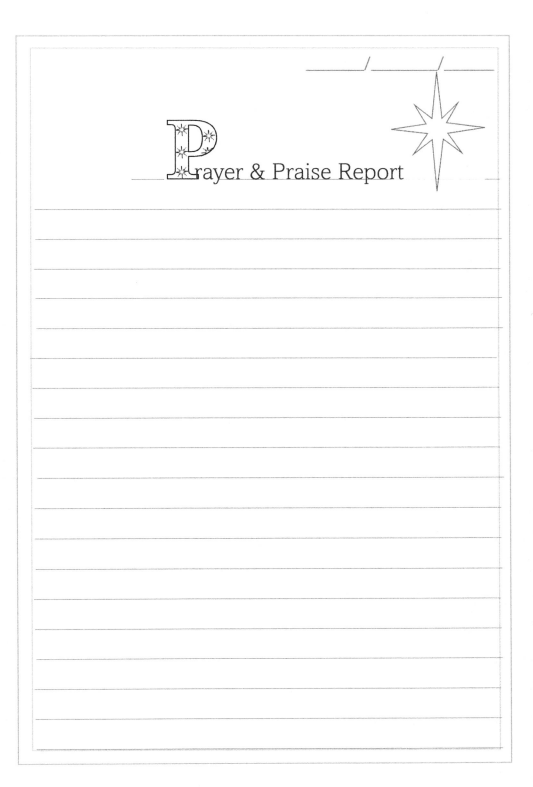

___/___

Prayer & Praise Report

_____/_____/_____

Do my friends and family celebrate me?

Scripture

___/___/___

Prayer

Scripture

____/____/____

Do friends and family celebrate when I have good success?

Scripture

Rejoice with them that do rejoice, and weep with them that weep. Romans 12:15

____/____/____

Do I Have Haters?

Scripture

Do I not hate those who hate you, LORD, and abhor those who are in rebellion against you? Psalm 139:21 NIV

___/___/___

Physical Support System
Who supports my day-to-day needs?
Am I showing them gratitude and thankfulness?

cripture

Rejoice always, pray continually, give thanks in all circumstances; for this is God's will for you in Christ Jesus
1 Thessalonians 5:16...

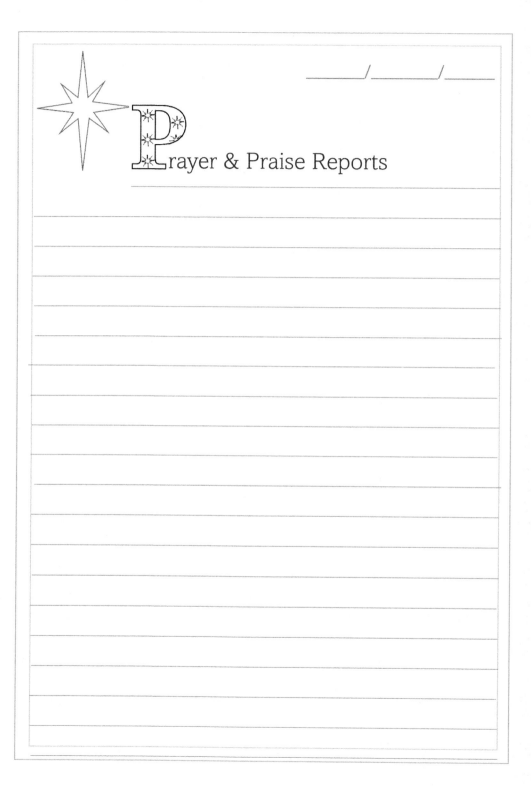

Prayer & Praise Reports

_____/_____/_____

_____/_____

Emotional Support System

Lord, you are the lifter of my head.

Scripture

He restores my soul; Psalm 23:3

Prayer

___/___

Scripture

_____/_____/_____

Spiritual Support System

Scripture

The spirit of a man will sustain him in sickness;
But who can bear a broken spirit? Proverbs 18:14

___/___/___

Prayer & Praise Reports

_____/_____/_____

Do I need to pray about or reconsider some friendships and relationships?

Scripture

___/___/___

Prayer & Praise Reports

____/____/____

Have I Met My Destiny Helpers?

Scripture

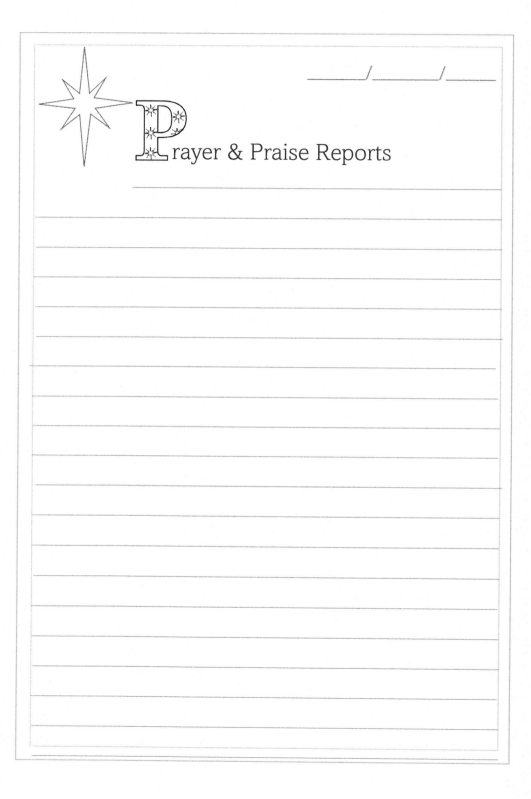

_____/_____/_____

Steps & Prayers to reach my education goals:

Scripture

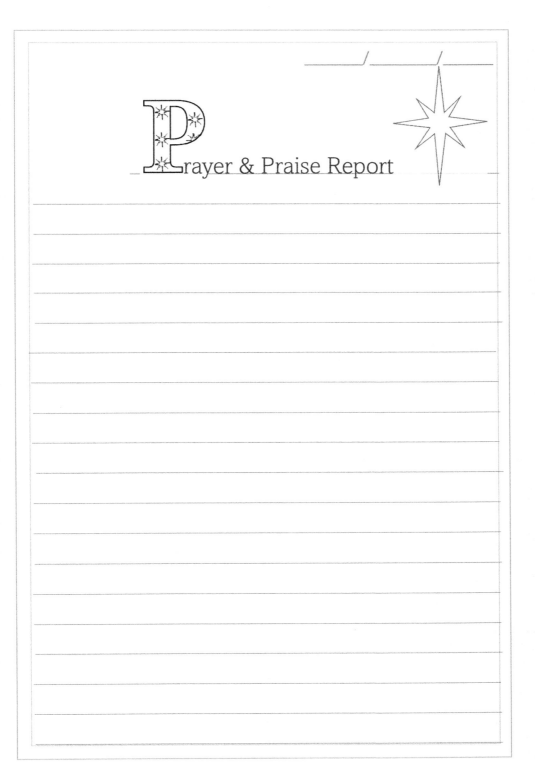

Prayer & Praise Report

_____/_____/_____

Steps & Prayers to reach my career goals:

Scripture

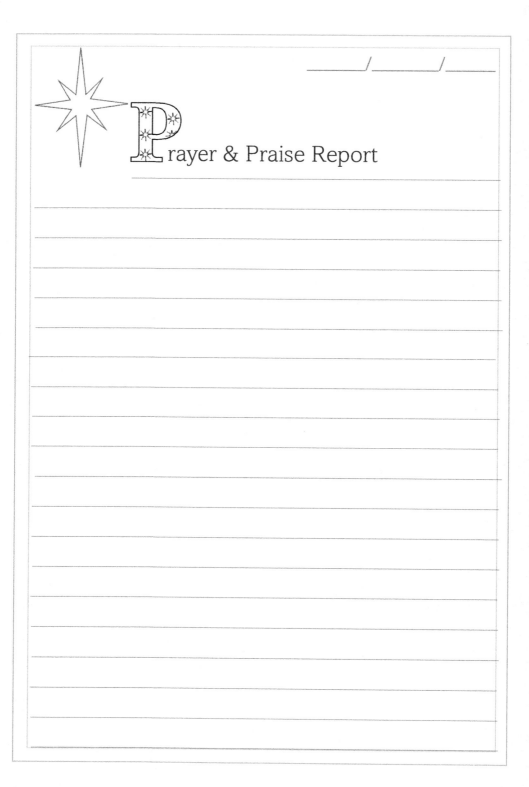

GOALS
This time next year…

Scripture

_____/_____/_____

GOALS
2 years from now...

Scripture

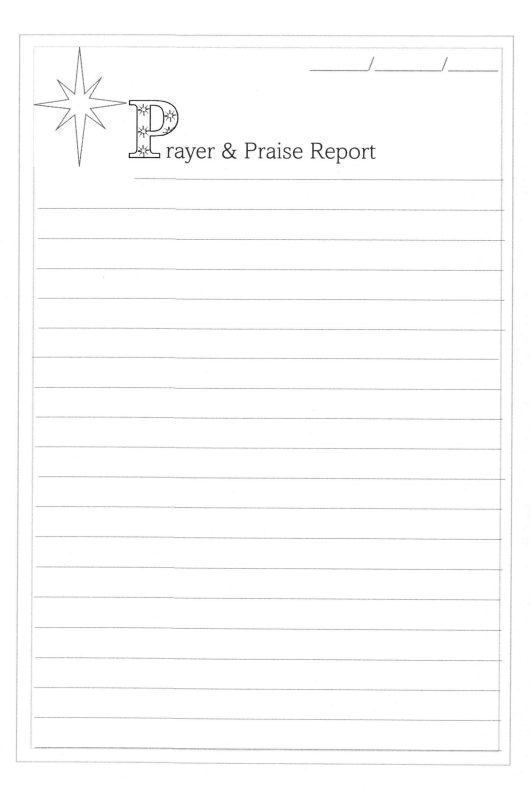

____/____/____

GOALS
5 years from now...

Scripture

___/___/___

Prayer & Praise Report

_____/_____/_____

GOALS
10 years from now...

Scripture

Prayer Requests & Notes

____/____

Scripture

____/____/____

GOALS
20 years from now...

Scripture

Prayer

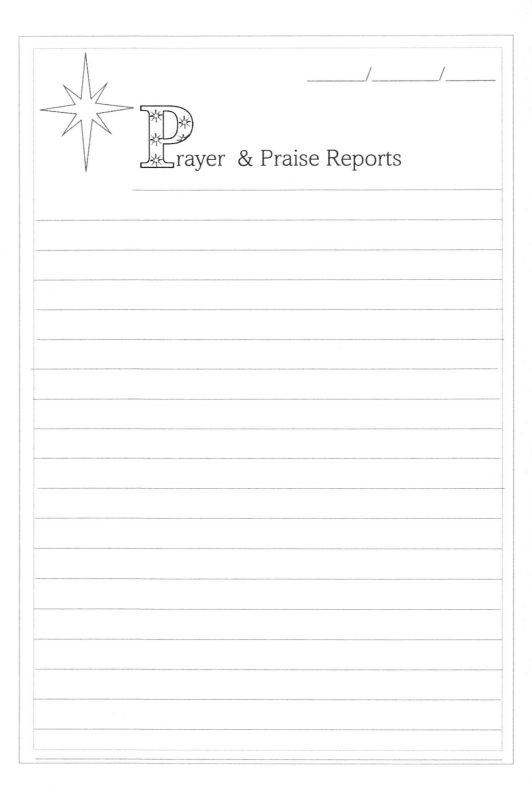

___/___/___

Prayer & Praise Reports

___/___/___

What type of person should I marry to fulfill my destiny?

Scripture

Prayer ____/____/____

Scripture

Prayer & Praise Report

___/___

_____/_____/_____

Steps & Prayers to reach my Marriage and Family goals:

Scripture

_____/_____/_____

Am I a physical support to anyone in this season? *If so, how am I doing?*

Scripture

____/____/____

Prayer

Scripture

___/___/___

Prayer & Praise Reports

_____/_____/_____

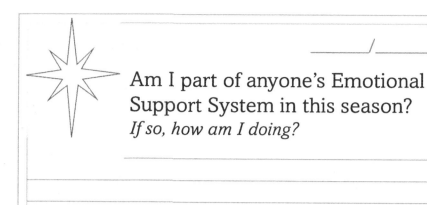

Am I part of anyone's Emotional Support System in this season?
If so, how am I doing?

Scripture

___/___/___

Prayer & Praise Reports

____/____/____

Am I a part of anyone's Spiritual Support system in this season?
If so, how am I doing?

Scripture

___/___/___

Prayer & Praise Reports

_____/_____/_____

Am I Anyone's Destiny Helper?
If so, whose? & *How Am I Doing?*

Scripture

___/___/___

Prayer & Praise Reports

____/____/____

Guarding My Star

Get Saved. Get Spirit-filled, Pray, Study the Word. Try not to sin. Keep good company and don't let negative people speak into your life.

Scripture

___/___/___

Prayer & Praise Reports

___/___/___

What I've Learned to Stay Away From

Stay away from evil people, the occult, people who practice in the occult, horoscopes, astrology, et cetera.

Scripture

The wise fear the LORD and shun evil, but a fool is hotheaded and yet feels secure. Proverbs 14:16

Prayer

___/___/___

I do not believe in astrology, I do not worship the sun, the moon, or the stars.

Scripture

Unfriendly Friends

_____/_____

Scripture

Prayer

___/___/___

Scripture

___/___/___

Prayer & Praise Reports

_____/_____/_____

Spiritual Protection Around My Star

Lord, put a hedge of protection around my star so it will not be hijacked or molested in the Name of Jesus.

Every evil star hunter, hands off my star, in the Name of Jesus.

Jealous friends and family, my star is not for you, Lord make it too hot for them to handle it in Jesus' Name.

___/___

Prayer

Scripture

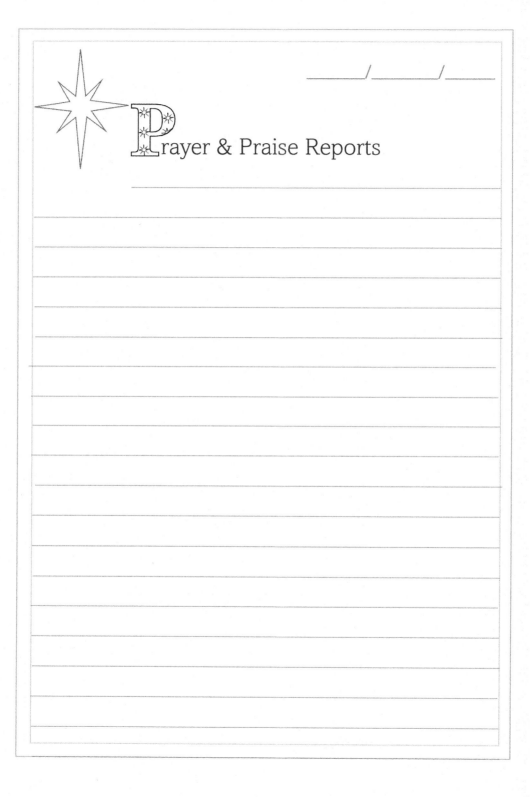

___/___/___

My Life and Success are Not to be played with.

My star is to help my destiny helpers find me; it is not for evil to find me. Any evil following my star, be cast away in the Name of Jesus.

I take my life, career, and success seriously to the Glory of God in the Name of Jesus.

Scripture

Prayer

_____/_____/_____

Scripture

Prayer & Praise Reports

___/___/___

_____/_____/_____

 My Life, Education, Career, Ministry, Marriage, and Family are Not For Sale.

Star hunters, traders, hijackers, get your evil eyes off my star! Angels of God poke out the eyes of any evil person or thing eyeing my star in Jesus' Name.

If my star comes up for sale on any evil market, Blood of Jesus cover it, hide it so no one can see it and return it to me, Amen.

cripture

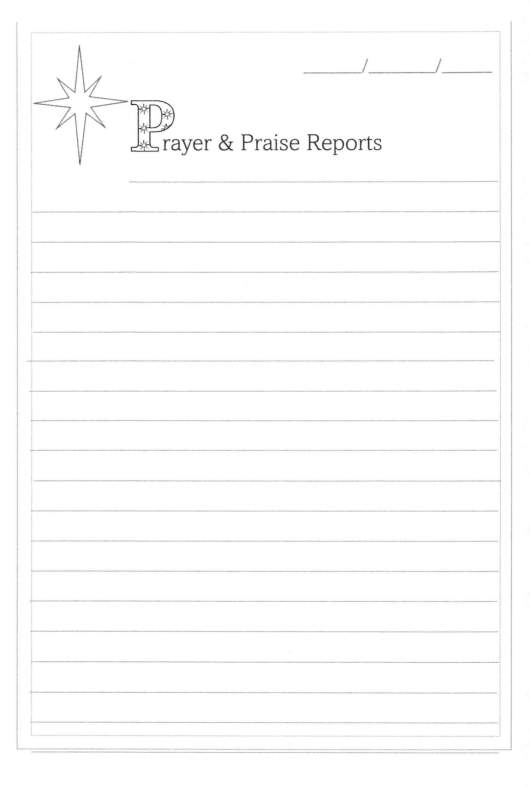

Rescuing My Star

Father, in the Name of Jesus I declare that any evil person or entity pointing at my star, I command their finger to wither right now.

Lord, I rescue my star from any evil pot, cage, prison, burial or other imprisonment in the Name of Jesus.

I take my star BACK from any evil person who is currently using MY star, in the Name of Jesus.

_____
_____
_____
_____
_____
_____
_____
_____
_____
_____

Scripture

___/___/___

Prayer & Praise Reports

_____/_____/_____

Uncaging My Star

Any evil holding my star, release it now in the Name of Jesus.

Every strongman guarding my star I send the angels of God to bind you and take you away to the abyss in the Name of Jesus.

Every cage door, every prison door, every cell door, every locked cage I command by the power of Christ that every lock be blown off and every door, gate, rock, stone, boulder be opened and removed in the Name of Jesus.

My Star, you are set free, Angels of the Lord, collect my Star and bring it out of captivity now in the Name of Jesus.

Scripture

___/___/___

Prayer & Praise Reports

____/____/____

Healing My Star

My star, for the damage you've sustained, I ask the Lord to wash you with Living Water in Jesus' Name.

My star be healed and be made whole again in the Name of Jesus.

My star, regain your strength and your purpose in my life in the Name of Jesus.

cripture

Prayer & Praise Reports

_____/_____/_____

Restoring My Star

_____/_____/_____

Any thing, person, entity or witchcraft power trying to dim tom star, I bind you in Jesus' Name and render you powerless.

Any covering over my star, not placed by the Lord Jesus Christ for protection, be burned off and removed forever in the Name of Jesus.

My star be infused with power by the Holy Spirit and shine, glow, twinkle in the Name of Jesus.

Scripture

___/___/___

Prayer & Praise Reports

____/____/____

Repositioning My Star

My star, if you ae wandering or floating aimlessly, come back into position now in the Name of Jesus.

God arise, and let my star find it's resting place in the Name of Jesus.

I am in Christ; my star belongs over me in the Name of Jesus.

cripture

____/____/____

Everybody Has A Star

There is one glory of the sun, another glory of the moon, and another glory of the stars; for *one* star differs from *another* star in glory. 1 Corinthians 15:41

cripture

You shall not covet … anything that belongs to your neighbor." Exodus 20:17 NIV

____/____/____

Prayer to Receive the Holy Spirit

Father, God I invite and receive the Holy Spirit in my life today. The Bible says that the Holy Spirit prays for me when I cannot pray for myself, when I'm going through the struggles of life, In discouragement, frustration oppressed or at a loss for words, When I don't even know what to say. When I'm down, when I'm lost, or feeling overcome, I need You LORD.

I invite and receive Your Spirit, Your Holy Spirit now in the Name of Jesus.

men

cripture

Made in the USA
Middletown, DE
14 October 2022

12506433R10070